Alice is half American and half German. She grew up in Bogota, Colombia, and attended the French and German School. Therefore, she is fluent in four languages. She has three children and seven grandchildren. In 1990, she was kidnapped in Colombia for 269 days and after regaining her freedom, she settled in Europe. Since then, she has travelled the world and immersed herself in the spiritual teachings of India, which she lives by. Through them, she has been able to live her Dharma or life's purpose by serving others. *Kidnapped* is her second published work.

I dedicate my story to all those who may find themselves in a difficult or similar situation in the hope that they might gain strength from it.

Alice Weil

KIDNAPPED

AUSTIN MACAULEY PUBLISHERS™

LONDON • CAMBRIDGE • NEW YORK • SHARJAH

A CIP catalogue record for this title is available from the British Library.

ISBN 9781528952392 (Paperback)
ISBN 9781528983624 (Hardback)
ISBN 9781528983631 (ePub e-book)

www.austinmacauley.com

First Published (2020)
Austin Macauley Publishers Ltd
25 Canada Square
Canary Wharf
London
E14 5LQ

To Stacy Thunes Krieger for her assistance in editing my work.

What Is Freedom?

Freedom is feeling the wind,
Seeing a blue sky,
Watching the sunset
And the clouds come and go.
It is not feeling fear,
It is being able to dream,
It is holding a hand,
It is going for a walk.
It is taking a nap,
Daydreaming by the sea,
It is sharing your life,
Being able to choose.
Freedom is in fact
The greatest gift of all.

Poem by Alice Weil

Foreword

Twenty-eight years after my rebirth as a free human being, I felt the urge to write the story of my life as it was in captivity, with the goal of creating an awareness of the willpower that is tucked away in all of us and of which we are not conscious. When the need arises, it stands by and allows us to master the most difficult situations that life may have in store. In sharing my story, I wish to give a ray of hope to all of those who might encounter a similar situation someday.

Prologue

She is known as Lili, and believe it or not, she owes this fact to her little sister who was unable to pronounce her proper name and shortened it to Lili. It's really her nickname, but sometimes when she is with her sisters and they call her Lili in front of their friends, they, too, call her Lili, not knowing any better. Her grandchildren also call her Lili, so as you can see, it has a lot of meaning for her. The sound of Lili is harmonious and she would even say it has a happy ring to it.

Lili had two things going for her: a very fine sense of humour and keen intuition. Her classmates at school would sometimes call her a witch, for whatever she said, always came true. This intuition never failed her. Being the eldest of five girls, and born into a prominent family, she always sensed that one day she would be kidnapped. Yes, that is the word…kidnapped. In those days, she used to smoke and therefore could not bear the thought of being kidnapped without having a pack of cigarettes, so she always made sure she had plenty in the car. A lot of good that did when the time came. But, dear Reader, I am getting ahead of myself so allow me to start from the beginning.

As I said, Lili's intuition never failed her and so, after having spoken her fears and anguish about not wanting to stay in Colombia, and not having been listened to, she went about her daily chores with a huge sense of unease, always expecting something to happen. When the day was over, she would invariably let out a sigh of relief, grateful that the unexpected had spared her once again. You could say it was a really weird situation.

She drove out to the farm one day, stopped at a gas station and filled up the car, bought an ice cream, then turned around

11

and went home. *Now, why did I do that?* she asked herself time and time again. It would not be until many months later, under completely different circumstances, that she would find the answer.

Then there was the issue of her daughter's fifteenth birthday. The persistent feeling that she would not be there to attend the party had her totally in its grip. So, when the important day finally came and went, and Lili was there with the rest of the family, she let out another huge sigh of relief. She asked herself out loud if her intuition could be sending the wrong messages.

"I certainly hope so!" she answered. But she was none too sure.

Life went on as usual and with every passing week, Lili was more and more convinced that her intuition had been playing tricks on her and that she had nothing to fear. What she didn't know was that she had only been granted some extra time. While in Europe for Christmas, she shared these fears with her family.

"No need to worry, they only kidnap men," she was told. If only they had known how mistaken they were.

Chapter 1

Lili returned from Europe, happy and carefree, going about her business, which partially consisted of driving out to the farm an hour's drive from the capital city, Bogota, to look after a few cows she had there. Those cows were really special and one, in particular, was quite a character. Her name was Paloma, which means pigeon in English. But she was definitely not the size of a pigeon. She was huge…and what an appetite she had.

Ripe bananas were her favourite and when Lili would enter the grass field with an armful of the ripe fruit, Paloma would follow her around like a shadow, not taking her eyes off of her. I cannot talk about the bananas without mentioning the carrots. This vegetable is very important, for it is said that if one feeds carrots to a cow, milk production increases.

Lili was so unconcerned about her safety, apparently having left her fears in Europe, that she stopped on her way to the farm to buy two sacks full of carrots at a carrot field, and have them loaded into her jeep. It had been a month since her return, and for once, she was not driving to the farm alone; she had company; a girlfriend and a plumber were with her.

On the summit of a nearby mountain, not far from the farm, was an important military post. Lili was happy, chatting and laughing as she drove on the narrow, winding road. Luckily, being a weekday, there was not much traffic. Then suddenly she slammed on the brakes.

"I nearly went through the windshield!" shouted her girlfriend.

"I'm awfully sorry, but do you see the checkpoint? Something must have happened over at the military post."

A soldier was holding an automatic weapon while a white Toyota blocked the road. Lili caught a glimpse of a blue truck. Holding her papers in her hand, she opened the car door and got out, as did her travelling companions. A man dressed in white trousers with a gun in his hand walked over to her and said, "A colonel of the army wants to speak to you. Your brother is suspected of drug trafficking."

Lili was stunned. "I'm sorry," she replied. "You must have the wrong person. I don't have a brother." This was beginning to scare her.

A very tall, mean looking man in the distance caught her attention. He was wearing heavy leather gloves and his hands were raised. Some cars pulled up behind hers, and the soldier signalled for the drivers to overtake and drive on. She tried to signal discreetly for one of them to stop and help her, but the soldier, and the man in the white trousers, told the driver of the car that stopped to mind his own business and step on the gas.

The white-trousers man moved in extremely close to her. Someone had turned the Toyota around and the motor was running. Lili dropped her car keys as she was lifted up forcibly and dumped on the floor of the Toyota. No sooner had the rear door slammed shut, the car started speeding down the highway. White-trousers man helped her to her feet and made her sit down next to him. He held a knife to her side. She looked around and retrieved her purse from the floor, and checked the contents.

Satisfied that nothing was missing, she turned to her companion and said, "You have me now, you can put that knife away."

The so-called soldier was sitting next to the driver, pointing his automatic weapon at her. Lili remembered her father once saying, "There is nothing more dangerous than a nervous person holding a weapon," so in a kind voice, she asked him to stop pointing his weapon at her since there was no need for it anymore. Much to her relief, he did as he was told.

14

Lili kept looking at the so-called soldier and thought there was something very strange about, him but couldn't put her finger on it which only added to her unease. On all military uniforms the name of the person wearing it is stitched above the left side pocket. Lili kept searching but the name was missing. The uniform was a fake. Then, she thought to herself, *I have been kidnapped...what I expected for so long has finally happened*, and she made up her mind there and then to put up no resistance. She would be calm and polite, well aware that her fate lay in their hands.

It took them almost all day to get to their destination. They drove to one part of the city and then to another and at some point, white-trousers got out and was replaced by a man wearing what looked like a very warm sweater. As he got in the truck, he said that the colonel had been delayed and if he did not arrive within a couple of hours, they would drive Lili back to where they picked her up. Lili just nodded her head. Her mind kept saying, *maybe I'm wrong and he might be telling the truth*, which gave her hope. They made one more stop and the driver got out and was replaced by someone else.

The mean-looking man wearing the gloves joined her in the back and sat on the bench facing her. Her heartbeat fast, her hands were sweating and she really needed to go to the bathroom. When she asked, she was told, "You will have to wait until you meet the colonel, and then you can go in his office."

Lili was desperate, but she knew she would have to wait. She was thirsty and when they offered her a bottle of Coca Cola, she refused, not trusting its contents. Lili lost track of time and had no idea how long they'd been driving when she was handed a pair of sunglasses, the inside of which had been covered with tape.

"Put them on and place your face in your lap," said the mean looking man. She glanced out the window one last time and took in her surroundings, then did as she was told. A garage door opened and the car drove in, then someone helped her out. The tape had been placed around the inside of the lenses so badly that she was able to see a staircase and a young girl standing next to it. She looked as if she had just come back from the hairdressers and wore a somewhat triumphant smile on her face.

Lili walked up the stairs with a heavy heart, her monkey mind keeping up its incessant chatter. She stood in front of a wall and a voice told her to get on all fours and crawl through the opening. She rebelled, "I don't want to."

"You must," said the voice.

"I have been kidnapped."

"You have," answered the voice.

No use putting up a fight, she thought, and with a very heavy heart, did as she was told. Deep down inside she had always known the truth, but being an eternal optimist, she had never given up hope that she might be wrong.

She crawled through the opening over to a doorway.

"Now crawl in there."

She hesitated for a moment then did as she was told. Once inside, she heard the person who had been following her close the gate and click the lock close. This would be her home from now on.

Chapter 2

She stood up and took in her surroundings. There were no windows, just two holes in one of the walls in which there was a fan in one and an extractor in the other. The space was very small and completely empty. The floor was covered in white foam that was concealed by a thick, white plastic. She turned her attention to the walls. The back and one of the sidewalls were made of concrete and the wall in which the extractor and fan were placed was made of wood. It was simply a partition that reached halfway across towards the entrance, which allowed her some privacy. Everything was covered in fibreglass and faded wallpaper and in some places, pages from old newspapers had been used, giving the impression that they had run out of said wallpaper. Lili looked at the dates on the newspapers: October to December 1989, and could tell nothing had been improvised and had been planned for some time. The noise from the fan and extractor were deafening, her ears were hurting and she wanted to scream for them to turn the machines off but realised that she was powerless and that her voice would be drowned out by the noise.

Like a wounded animal, she moved to the far end of the room, or cell as it shall be called from here on, and closed her eyes. The voice became louder, *you are not kidnapped, you are not kidnapped...* But since it was unbearable to listen to, she would open her eyes. *Yes, you are. Yes, you are.* Someone standing at the entrance interrupted her and opened the lock. The one in the heavy sweater, now wearing a face mask, brought in a mattress, some bed linens, a blanket, a chamber pot and a roll of toilet paper before leaving.

She looked at the chamber pot in utter disgust and disbelief, understanding that she was being reduced to a caged animal. She, at least, would be able to relieve herself, and smiled at the thought of her jailer having to empty it out, then went about putting the mattress in place and making her bed. She had barely finished when the sweater man returned. Even though she was scared and anguished, keeping a clear head was important so as not to allow her emotions to get the better of her.

Having expected this situation for so long, Lili had had time to prepare for it. She went to the doorway and said: "I will not ask you your name, for you will surely lie to me and I cannot live with lies, therefore I shall give you a name. I will call you John. I realise that I am in your hands and I will not put up a fight. We will be polite and civil to each other, for it is in all of our best interests." He agreed, and taking the chamber pot with him, informed that he would return.

Lili looked at the roll of toilet paper and had an idea. She would mark each passing day with a little piece of the paper, which she would hide underneath her mattress. That way, she would know exactly the amount of days she had spent here as well as the date, which she memorised by repeating it several times to herself, 'Wednesday 7 February.'

John returned with a gallon of water and some food. He informed her that the light would be turned off at 10 pm and would come back on at 6 am the next morning. No, she could not have a flashlight, he mumbled under his breath, and then something about her getting used to it. He then, asked her to please hand over her watch before leaving again. She did as she was told without saying a word and was very much aware that things were turning out just as she had imagined.

She decided that when the light went out, she would have to devise a way of finding her chamber pot, water and mattress since she would not be able to see anything in the pitch dark. So, using her arms, she measured the distance between the wall and her mattress and the distance between the end of her mattress and the chamber pot. After rehearsing this several times, she knew exactly how many arm lengths lay between one thing and another. Then she resigned herself to having to sleep in the clothes she was wearing as she had no clothes to change into.

Having nothing more to do, her monkey mind resumed its incessant chatter. It jumped from one subject to the other, giving her no respite whatsoever. She felt lost, cold and as her thoughts wandered back to her three children, her eyes welled with tears. They would be home by now and she was sure their father would have told them the truth. *How would they have reacted to it?* She wondered. The pain she felt at imagining their anguish was almost too much to bear. She made a vow right then that they would not be a part of this ordeal, she would not bring them or anyone else into her living hell. She knew that she would succeed and succeed she did—but her success was not immediate.

As announced, the light went out and it went pitch black. She lay curled up on her mattress and all of a sudden realised how lucky she was to have given up smoking some months before. Everything around her was highly flammable and she was sure that her jailers would have refused to provide her with cigarettes. The fan and extractor were turned off and she was thankful for the silence. She was very much aware of being in the hands of criminals and was filled with anguish, not knowing what they might be capable of doing to her. She listened intently, trying to identify whatever noises she heard but eventually fell into a restless sleep.

Chapter 3

It was still dark when she woke up the next morning. She waited impatiently until they turned on the light, the fan and extractor. It must have been around 6 am when that finally happened. Relieved, she went back to sleep but was woken up by John asking from the doorway if she was alright and informed her before departing that someone would bring her breakfast a little later.

The night before they had brought her a toothbrush and some toothpaste. She brushed her teeth but then realised there was no washbasin or running water to rinse it with. *We take these little daily details for granted and only realise their importance when we don't have them anymore*, she thought to herself. She made up her mind to give the brush to whomever came in next to be rinsed out for her. Making her bed gave her something to do, and it was then that she came up with the idea that the mattress would be her bedroom and the corridor between the mattress and the gate would be her living room.

She curled up in that narrow space and allowed her mind to wander, reliving every single activity her husband and children might be doing at that time. She could see her husband driving off to work, the kids waiting for the school bus…it was agony. Being alive and yet not being with them because her freedom had been taken from her by other human beings. She was held in a cage like an animal. It's almost like being dead, for one is no longer with them, yet one is alive but completely powerless. Only death could relieve her of the agonising pain she was feeling, but she had a duty towards her family, as well as herself, to stay alive so she resolved to stop thinking about her family's daily routine.

Her chatter was then interrupted by John bringing breakfast. The dishes were neatly laid out on a big wooden tray. He opened the gate and slid it inside, then of course closed and locked it. She hated that sound. It kept reminding her that she was a prisoner. She wasn't at all hungry, but not knowing when she would be served her next meal, decided not to let the yoghurt and cereal go to waste. When she finished, she studied the tray and decided that since the floor was so soft, she would walk on it to keep her feet in good shape.

When John returned to pick up the empty dishes, he asked her to please make a list of contacts so they could establish a connection with her family. This placed Lili amid a huge dilemma. What right did she have to give out her contacts' names unbeknownst to them, placing them at risk? What they were demanding was so very wrong, but on the other hand it was probably the only way they had to make contact, even though she was not too convinced. In the end, she decided that she could not and would not name her family and that it had to be someone unrelated to her. After mulling it over for a long time, she decided to give them the name of her friend's husband. She had been a witness to her kidnapping and she was sure Jacob was very well informed.

For hours on end, she was left to her own devices. She discovered that if she sat on the chamber pot, she could hear what was going on in the room next door, and thus was able to confirm that John and the girl, the one who had met her when she arrived, could see her through the holes of the fan and extractor. Her suspicions were confirmed when she heard John say, "She is sleeping."

The girl, whom she called Rose, interrupted Lili's train of thought by asking her what she would like to have for lunch. Being very keen on confirming where she was, she asked for a pizza from Pizza Hut and a doughnut, then heard a motorcycle leave and shortly thereafter, return. Rose opened the gate and gave her what she had requested. Lili put two and two together and deduced she was being held in the city, not far from a shopping centre. In addition to John and Rose there was the motorcyclist, so for the time being she was aware of three people in the house. I forgot to mention, she had no idea what anyone actually looked like, as they all wore face masks in her presence.

Rose came in and spent the rest of the afternoon with her. She told her that she was very good at martial arts and Lili could tell by her hands that she was very young. Then Lili had an idea. She would teach Rose how to knit, which would give her something to do. Fairly certain that John was in command, he would be the one to see to it that she did not run out of wool. Rose was delighted but told her that she would have to talk to John about it first. Lili then asked Rose for a bowl, so she could wash her hands and it was agreed that it would only be emptied twice a day. What a luxury it was to finally be able to wash her hands.

John came by late that night and positioned himself in the corridor outside her gate. Lili sat down in her living room. He again inquired about the contact and she gave him a name. "Just one?" he asked with a sneer.

"Sorry, I'm afraid I don't know anyone else who would risk their life for me."

He handed her some sheets of paper and dictated a letter he would send to Jacob.

When she finished, she handed the letter to him, saying she would keep the rest of the paper as she wanted to journal. He also agreed to her knitting idea.

Just as he was getting up to leave, she asked him for a Bible. This was not from a religious standpoint, however, but a practical one. She had always wanted to read it and now there was time to do so. Before leaving he said, "You have ten minutes, then the lights will go out," and wished her a goodnight.

The irony, thought Lili. *How could anyone have a good night in a place like this?* As she curled up on her mattress, she realised that she'd been wearing the same clothing for at least three days and was beginning to smell. She also felt grateful that at least now her family would be informed she was still alive. Luckily, her kidnapping was not politically motivated but instead economically, so her chances of coming out of the ordeal, alive, were bigger than had it been the other way around.

The next morning, true to his word, John installed a bell on the wall near her mattress and they devised a code. If she rang once, it meant she needed something and if she rang twice, it meant they should turn the fan and extractor on or off. Since Lili had also complained about the poor light, he installed another lamp on the partition wall.

After lunch, Rose paid her an unexpected visit. She brought knitting needles and wool with her, saying she was eager to learn, then sat down next to her and received the first lesson. Lili was really happy, for now she had something to entertain herself with, as well as the knowledge that by teaching Rose how to knit, her supply of wool would not run out. Rose learned very quickly and Lili suggested she make a sweater for herself. She happily agreed. Lili was still very much intrigued by her jailers. She pried Rose with subtle questions: "Who are they? What group do they belong to?" Yet, though Rose had no formal education, she was very much streetwise. After a couple of hours, Rose excused herself and left, telling Lili that if she wanted to continue knitting, she could, "My sweater won't take as long if I have some help." Lili was very happy to oblige.

As the days went on, she began adapting to her new life, trusting nobody, always watchful and alert. They now offered tea with her meals and she gladly accepted. For one, it was a way of saving water as the conditions were similar to living under siege; she never knew if they would continue to provide her with the gallon bottles and the paper cups, she drank her tea from. Speaking of the cups, they were very useful for rinsing her toothbrush, she discovered. She would hold it over the cup and pour water over it, and that worked well for her

As she lay curled up in her 'living room', she took an inventory of all the ways and means she had found to solve the lacks and the have-nots. She smiled and said to herself out loud, "*This is one way to increase and bring out the potential stored in every human being,*" then added bitterly, "*but there are certainly less cruel ways to accomplish the same thing.*"

Chapter 4

One evening, John showed Lili a small transistor radio. She was delighted, as she would now be able to listen to the news, know what time it was, and listen to music. Her joy was short lived because John made it very clear that she could choose only one radio station, and the radio would be out of her reach. She gave him the station name and by asking the frequency, it confirmed he had never heard of it, but he left her to enjoy the music.

She listened intently and it was not long before they mentioned the time of day and the date. Lili was ecstatic as she counted her little pieces of toilet paper to find they were correct. Not one single day had she lost track of. Her only worry now was that John would find out she was aware of the time. One of their goals was to make her lose all sense of time and place, that she knew, but this was definitely not going to happen. All those little details gave her a sense of being in control and she felt proud of herself.

That evening marked the beginning of John's nightly visits. He would come at 10 pm, sit in the corridor outside her cell with the gate open, while Lili on her side of the gate, and they would have a chat.

During the conversations, she tried incredibly hard to keep a blank expression, but this was proving hard for her, as she had a very expressive face.

He told her that initially they had chosen her husband as their victim but came to the conclusion that it would be a lot easier if they took her instead, since her husband would then be able to negotiate her release. Lili made no comment and tried her best not to show any surprise. He also told her that they had been following her for a long time, thus confirming her intuition that this should have happened before her daughter's birthday but had successfully eluded them when she left the country.

Yes, thought Lili. *I was right all along.* She continued to listen to him but said nothing. Noticing her indifference, he asked her what books she would like to read. She told him she would not like to look back at the time spent here as wasted and would he therefore, consider getting her some books on law from the university? He turned off the radio and said he would have to ask the boss before wishing her a goodnight.

Sitting on the chamber pot, Lili listened intently and tried to pick up whatever sound she was able to hear. She could make out John and Rose's voices but there was another, third voice. *Could it be the motorcyclist?* She wondered. With this thought on her mind, she fell into a restless sleep, but a noise outside her gate woke her up shortly thereafter. Was somebody watching her? Were they going to come in and harm her? She was extremely frightened and her whole body started to shake. No use screaming for help, she decided, and made believe she was sleeping soundly.

Lili had never felt so vulnerable or helpless in her life. She was completely at the mercy of these people, whoever they were. They had no conscience and no scruples. In fact, they were monsters. The day after they brought her there, John had told her in a very severe tone of voice, "Do not pray that the police or the army will find you, because if they do, rest assured you will be the first to die." Lili had taken that warning to heart.

As soon as she woke up the next day, she rang the bell and they turned on the fan and extractor. She also hoped that someone would come and turn on the radio so she could get an idea of the time. John entered, asking if she'd had a restful sleep (so cynical, she thought) then turned on the radio.

Rose surprised her with two pairs of pyjamas, some underwear and socks. She also brought her a bra, which was too big so Lili returned it to her. The fact is, Lili was completely flat chested and she knew it had been a reaction to the shock. Very grateful for the clean clothing, she changed and Rose said she would take her clothes and wash them. Even though she had not showered in days, Lili felt much better. She had one problem however…she was very cold. On his nightly visit, Lili complained to John about it and he returned with a warm sweater, which he said she could have.

Lili had never worn another people's clothing. Being the eldest, she'd had the privilege of having everything new and her sisters were the ones who wore hand-me-downs, but she was so cold that she thankfully accepted the offer and put it on. John had been right. Certain situations in life force a person to surrender and be humble. This was one of them.

Very keen on finding out who this John person was, Lili pried him with questions. He told her that she had never witnessed the poverty of the city since she was confined to the rich areas, but there were people who were very poor. The money he made when he'd held a decent job wasn't even enough to pay for groceries. He wanted to become rich quick and had been offered a job as a drug dealer, which he refused because it was too risky, so he agreed to join a gang that specialised in kidnappings. It was fast money with little risk involved. John told her to remember that she was an investment and the merchandise had a price. Once the price was agreed on and the money received, she would be released. She listened to him, trying to be as expressionless as possible and without interrupting, then he ended his monologue by telling her it would probably be the beginning of August before that happened.

This information did not upset Lili, for she had always known that she was in it for a very long time. He also told her that he had consulted with his boss and that she should forget about studying law during her captivity. She simply said she was disappointed and as she said this, he handed her a few books in Spanish. When he left, she took a closer look at them. There was a book on South American literature with short stories written by different authors, one by Victor Hugo and a Bible that bore a seal of some missionary mission on the first page.

John's story of them being a gang that specialised in kidnappings did not make any sense. The books pointed to educated individuals and she was certain that the people who made up gangs were not. A dreadful thought came to her: *what if they were members of the Guerrilla?* She was very much aware that if this were the case, her probability of coming out alive was very slim. She quickly dismissed the thought, as it caused her quite a bit of anguish, so she convinced herself that they were just a gang.

At night she could hear them walking, making their rounds. They were much organised. At about 8 am, the activity would begin and Lili would listen to them talking, even though she could not make out what they were saying. She would hear the car drive off, the garage door close with a bang and, with the exception of the noise the motorcycle made, everything went very quiet.

Lili had been apprehensive about what would happen on the weekends. Fridays had a reputation for people going out to party and getting drunk. *How would her jailers behave?* She wondered. She needn't have worried, as they were very disciplined, and the weekends were just like any ordinary day.

Then one Friday, something really scary happened. John came to her gate and told her in a whisper that they would not be turning on the fan or extractor. He disconnected the bell and all she would have was the light. There should be no noise whatsoever and he would let her know when things got back to normal, saying it had to do with something on the outside. She curled up in her living room, hoping nothing would happen, and could hear them moving furniture on the floor above. Then all of a sudden everything went quiet. John came, armed, and stood outside her gate.

Lili was really frightened but continued to knit, which took her mind off the situation in which she was living. She heard someone knock twice on the front door but the summons was left unanswered. After a while, John left and she could hear him whispering to Rose in the room next door. Three hours later, John came and told her everything was back to normal and asked what she would like to eat. Lili was very keen to know if there had been communication with the outside world, so she asked for a hamburger and to her relief, she heard the motorcycle leave and shortly thereafter, Rose brought one in for her.

Outside communication was very important, it meant they could send and receive messages to Lili's husband's friend, but she soon found out that this was wishful thinking. She continued writing in her journal, as there was always something to write about. One morning she read back to the first pages and noticed how unsteady her handwriting had been, the letters small and uneven. Yet, as the days went on and she calmed down, her handwriting became normal again. *The body projects what goes on in the mind.*

John and Rose had been taking turns looking after her. One day a very tall, lean guy brought her some breakfast and informed her that he would be taking care of her from that day on. Aware of having breathed in nothing but stale, dry air, Lili asked if he could bring her a pot of hot water in which eucalyptus leaves had been boiled. He obliged, and this really helped her. She was becoming very grateful for these small things.

Chapter 5

In one of their nightly chats, John told Lili how much money her family was offering for her. She could sense someone listening in on the conversation, at the entrance to her cell and this made her very uneasy, but her expression remained blank as she said, "If my husband were the one locked up in here instead of me, I wouldn't even offer half that amount."

"At this rate, only God knows when you'll be released," John said in an angry voice. As soon as he left, Lili laughed softly to herself. She'd made her point. If they, whoever they were, thought they could bargain with her as well, she had nipped that idea swiftly in the bud. Happy knowing they were in contact with her family, at least now they knew she was alive, even though they fully ignored her whereabouts and the conditions she was being held in. She settled in even more for the long haul. She was prepared to wait and would not despair, even learning to surrender to the knowledge that life would go on as usual for her family and accept that she had no influence over it. It was a power struggle between her jailers and her family and she knew that, but her responsibility was towards her family and she was determined to not let them down and allow herself to be broken by these monsters.

From time to time, one of them would ask her the date and day of the week to see if she had lost her sense of time but, much to their distress, her replies were always correct. One night, John told her that all communication had been broken off and he urgently needed another list of contacts. She was crestfallen but she did not show it. In a business-like manner, she told him that she would need her address book, which was in her purse. He obliged and left her to write the list. Going through the names she felt very lonely, for the contacts were all friends of her husband or father's, and aside from her sisters, she realised she had no acquaintances of her own.

With a very heavy heart she handed the list to John who then asked for her address book back as well. *What could he want it for?* she wondered. *Why make a list if they already have the information?* It didn't make sense, but nothing seemed to make sense in her circumstances anyway, so she did not dwell on it for too long.

A couple of weeks later, sometime in March, John told her that communications had been restored. This filled her with joy, for in the back of her mind she was constantly imagining the anguish her family must be feeling at the lack of news. Realising that there was a channel of communication again, she remembered that inside her address book was a lab receipt for a urine exam, her son had taken. She asked John to please have the receipt delivered so the results could be picked up. He told her in no uncertain terms that this was not possible then took it from her and tore it up.

Lili felt her eyes well with tears, but brushed them quickly aside not willing to show any weakness. The sheer torture of not knowing how her children were faring was indescribable. Every time her thoughts went to her father, who was seriously ill, she felt a terrible pain in her heart, as if she were being stabbed with a knife. But even though she knit, read and tried to distract her mind, the pain only subsided—it never left. Only death could put an end to the pain she was enduring, for once one had transcended, all thoughts and feelings would cease to exist. The worst torture for someone being held against their will is the inability to shut off all emotions, living with all the unanswered questions.

Lili weighed her options. She had long conversations, with herself, about this. Putting an end to her nightmare crossed her mind many times, but was also aware that she was being challenged and she was no coward. There was no way she would do the dirty work for them. Her responsibility towards her family was also huge and she was certain they were doing everything in their power to get her out, so it would be unfair to them to give up.

31

The chats with John gave her something to look forward to. He was well read, he loved weapons and when he spoke about them his eyes lit up. They talked about music, history and geography. One day Lili suggested he buy her a *Time Magazine* so she could translate the articles for him as he did not speak English. He thought it was a great idea. Now Lili had one more thing to keep her busy, as well as staying informed about what was going on in the world. When John brought her a huge writing block and some pens, it guaranteed her supply of paper and pens.

One evening, John picked up the radio to turn it off as usual but Lili gave him a pleading look and asked if he would please let her have it. He hesitated for a couple of minutes then handed it to her under the condition that if he should ever ask for it back, she would return it. She wholeheartedly agreed. You can't imagine, dear Reader, how much that little transistor radio changed Lili's life. It gave her access to the world. Now she was able to listen to the news, discovering radio stations with different programmes, listening to classical music and various debates on a variety of topics, which all helped to quiet her monkey mind.

In the early hours of one particular morning, she heard some noise coming from the entrance to the corridor that led to her cell. Listening intently, she realised they were doing something to the door at that end. They worked on it for a long time and it took her some time to figure out that they had fixed it in such a way that it no longer made a sound when it was opened. This meant she wouldn't be warned anymore when someone was coming. That night she was again awoken by a noise coming from her gate and was sure someone was standing there, gazing at her. She lay very still, making believe she was sound asleep and indeed must have dozed off, for she did not hear the person leave.

The following morning, she decided to change her sleeping pattern, sleeping during the day and staying awake at night. This way, she could spend the night curled up in her living room and no one would be able to see her there, as well as being able to hear if someone came in. This decision made her feel less vulnerable and it worked wonders on her spirit, listening to the nightly concerts as if she were in her own private concert hall. Her heart filled with gratitude towards her mother who had not only taught her how to keep herself busy, but instilled a love of music in her. But while she felt gratitude, there was a deep sadness, knowing her mother was suffering as well. Yet, in contrast to her father, she was in fine health.

On another day, John, wearing gloves, came and brought a tape recorder with him. He told her that communication had been restored, and they had orders from the boss to send proof that Lili was alive. She did not bother asking how they were going to do this, as she knew her question would remain unanswered. He gave her a text to read, saying she was not allowed to change or add anything. It was no easy task trying to read it in a steady voice. After having her repeat it several times, he was finally satisfied.

Lili cried most of that night, thinking about her children hearing their mother's voice and being confronted with reality again. They were motherless and the outcome was a huge question mark. As the days went by, her perception of what had been her outside world slowly began to shift. Her life of freedom faded with time and she became more and more focused on her present state: The Now. There was no past, as it was silently slipping away, and no future, either. It was simply living by the day. She had nowhere to go, but had things to do, so she made up a schedule of knitting, reading and translating.

One day, she had asked John for her watch, but he refused to give it to her, saying that knowing the time of day would be of no use to her and would only increase her anguish. After having a couple of conversations with herself on the matter, she had to admit it made sense.

Lili had always been very disciplined and she made a point of sticking to a routine. She would wake up, make her bed, brush her teeth and spit the contents into the chamber pot (disgusting as it was) then wash herself as best as she could before reading one of her favourite psalms from which she got the courage to face her jailers. Then she would ring for her breakfast.

Solitary confinement allowed Lili to meet a very good acquaintance: Herself. She decided to call this her witnessing awareness and knew they were very close and inseparable. They had no secrets between them and they shared everything. It was certainly her most enriching experience and dear Reader, we have remained together ever since.

Lili need not have worried about her children listening to the tape. To her great disappointment and despair, John told her that the tape had not and would not be delivered and refused to give her a reason. With time, she succeeded in hiding her emotions very well. The lack of reaction from her always infuriated him and his response would be to either leave immediately or threaten her with something. This time it was a threat: From now on, she would have to wash her underwear in the same bowl she used to wash her hands. Lili flatly refused and asked for some panty liners. She was very much surprised when he brought her a box.

Lili resolved that she would not let them wash her pyjamas. Who cared if they were dirty or they stank? She had not had a shower in weeks anyway, and since she couldn't do anything about it, it didn't bother her. Her captors were the ones who had to live with the stench.

Chapter 6

These events marked a turning point. Her jailers became less caring and even more indifferent to her plight. She was told that she had to save her drinking water, which she already did unbeknownst to them. She would write on the gallon jug the date she had received it and when it was three quarters full, she would ask John for more. Now she made a point of drinking less and waiting to ask for a new one until it was half-empty. She'd finished knitting Rose's sweater but when she was halfway through, offered to knit John a sweater and a blanket. Believe it or not, he brought her the full amount of wool she'd asked for.

Lili rationed everything. She would ask for batteries for her radio after two weeks and four weeks later she would not put in the new ones but the old ones she had taken out, which usually gave her a week more of battery life. She could not bear the thought of not being able to listen to her programmes. She began to knit just 10 rows a day, thus saving wool, and she translated a paragraph or two a day and only two weeks after she received the first copy of *Time Magazine*, she requested the next one. It was like living under siege, fully well aware that she depended on her jailers for her provisions and the mood and state of mind the boss and his partners were in. She hoarded chocolates, toilet paper and chips for, dear Reader, she couldn't just run out to a store and purchase what she needed. Understanding the plight of a caged animal, she also realised the full dependency of an infant on its mother. Her survival depended on the whim of others.

As she lay curled up in her bedroom during the day, her thoughts went back to the time she had visited Dachau. Yes, this was her Dachau. The thought was so painful that she did not allow herself to elaborate more on it, but this memory has stayed with her ever since.

On the days that Rose came in to keep Lili company, she would talk a great deal. She told her that she had been a street urchin with no education and that now she made her living taking care of kidnapped people. Men were the worst to take care of and when they gave her too much trouble, she had different ways of dealing with them, such as chaining them to the bed or whatever. Lili found her cruel and she couldn't stand her vulgar vocabulary. Shortly before the so-called 'good times' came to an end, she complained to John, and he replaced her with the lean, tall guy who had brought her the pot of eucalyptus water.

He, too, told her his story. After being fired from his job in a cocaine lab, he was offered this one, which he didn't hesitate to take as it was less risky and paid more money. According to him, his buddies did not trust each other and said that at the rate the negotiations were moving, she would be here for a long time. But he suggested she could speed things up by setting a price herself. Lili pretended not to hear the question and he did not repeat it. Sometimes when the despair would creep up on her, she would tell herself: *If my husband knew of the kind of people, I am a cohabitant with, he might speed things up.* To which her reluctant mind would reply: *I am fairly sure he knows you are not living amongst nuns.*

Lili was told one evening that the fan would be turned on at 7 am and turned off at 11 pm. They had used the money she'd had in her purse to pay for the clothing they brought her and were not prepared for the negotiations to take this long. They were running out of money and therefore, she would have to eat the food they prepared for her and if she did not like, well, she could just go without. She was actually quite relieved. No longer having to think about what she wanted to eat was one less worry. However, they did continue to provide her with her chips and chocolates.

Lili made herself a diary and every time John told her that there had been a communication, or that the communication had been broken, she would make a mark on it. This allowed her some insight into their way of operating and it also kept her mind active. Several weeks had gone by since the new measures were put in place and one morning John informed her that the partners decided Lili was to have a shower.

She was not at all overjoyed at the news, since she had been warned that if she made any false movements or if the army or police appeared, she would be shot. Her eyes had to be covered with a thick bandage and she was to crawl under the gate out the opening, guarded by Rose and John the entire time who were both armed. After she entered the bathroom and stepped into the shower, she was told to face the wall. The shower curtain was drawn and the bandage removed, after which she would undress and turn on the water. Everything she needed was at hand. Rose, of course, remained in the bathroom.

Lili loved the feeling of water on her skin but the enjoyment was short lived. Soon they demanded she get dressed and when she had to crawl under the first gate, she felt anger rising inside her. When she crawled through her own gate into the living room and heard the gate close and the lock click into place, she swore she would never ever accept their invitation to shower again. The humiliation and realisation of her cruel situation made her feel such rage that it undermined the benefits. After this, she asked John for a scourer. He obliged, and from then on, she washed herself with it as best she could. The thought of it doing away with her cellulite brought a smile to her face.

Her little radio was a curse as well as a blessing. She listened to her programmes, which she very much enjoyed and helped to quiet her monkey mind. But it also became a curse; when listening to the morning news she heard of the bombs that had gone off at a shopping mall. The military had taken control of the city. She would have given anything to be kept in the dark about this, but that not being the case, she worried frantically about her family and relatives, hoping against hope that none of them had been hurt.

John came in that evening and confirmed her worst fears. They had to lay low, which meant they were cut off from the outside world. The power was shut off daily, which only served to agitate her jailers. On those occasions, one of them would stand guard outside her cell gate, an automatic weapon in his hands. No sounds were made and her jailers spoke in whispers. John explained to her that if the police or army were making a house search, the first thing they'd do was to shut off the power. The lights would sometimes be out for the whole day. She dreaded this. Not only was it pitch black around her, but if she had to use the chamber pot, she would have to endure the smell because she could not call anyone.

She asked John several times for a flashlight but he refused, saying she might use it to signal with and it was too much of a risk for them to take. So she would sit on the blanket she was knitting. It was so long and wide it served as a cushion, minding the knitting needles of course, or she would curl up in the bedroom and listen to her different programmes.

Her time was spent learning about music, farming and listening to the national and international news. There was a whole repertoire, which took up the entire night, hearing her jailers make their rounds. At about 6.30 am, the garage door would open and the car would leave returning just before 6 pm. She could tell if it was a sunny or a gloomy day by looking through the holes in the fan. To her amazement, one time as she was looking up at the ceiling, she discovered that it worked like a mirror with the sunlight, and she could see the reflections of the people who were in the room next door. This was a great discovery and it kept her very much entertained, as well as confirming her suspicions that she was being observed. Her jailers had their routine and she had hers.

Someone would leave in the car on Saturdays to do the grocery shopping and on those days, her lunch always arrived late. By Thursday, her meals would decrease in size. The days Lili disliked most were Saturdays and Sundays. They seemed to drag on forever. The radio programmes were very boring and so she would bury her nose in a book or just sleep. On Sundays, everyone would leave and only one person would stay to keep an eye on her. The senses are truly amazing and her sense of hearing increased so much that she could make out the slightest noise.

Since changing her sleeping routine, unbeknown to her jailers who thought she was sleeping longer hours, Lili was able to control everything. She could tell if they had opened the gate leading to her cell because she would receive more light and that there was a bunk bed in the room next to her wall partition. John slept on top, him jumping off the bed, every morning, had given him away, and Rose slept on the bottom bed. One day they got into a terrible fight and he hit her. To be honest, dear Reader, her cries did not move Lili's heart. *Have I become insensitive?* she asked herself. The truthful answer was that Lili was becoming indifferent.

The new sleeping pattern and spending the night in her living room also allowed her to not only to listen to her nightly programmes, but be vigilant and always prepared. Convinced that their prey was sleeping, her captors were not concerned whatsoever about the noise they made, which allowed Lili to have an insight in to their daily activities around the house.

The incident with the terrorist attack was soon forgotten, the military patrols stopped and, according to John, the communications with her family had been restored. There was only one hitch and he repeated this quite often: the bargaining was very slow. Lili did not understand at first, and then he made it clear that if her family did not raise the offer considerably, they, her kidnappers, would be forced to take drastic action. John showed her several weapons, including a hand grenade, and told her that if necessary, they had various ways and means to make hard-headed individuals understand who held the cards. This statement only increased Lili's anguish and she listened intently to the news.

A couple of weeks later, John informed her that he was going to take her radio away since they were going to have to do something drastic and it would surely be in the news. She told him very sweetly that she would probably not even hear about it, as she was sleeping a great deal. He thought for a minute and agreed to let her keep her companion, but warned that if she did happen to hear something, she was to keep it to herself. She gave him her word.

It was not long before she heard over the radio that a rocket had been fired in a part of the city. No name was given, just the address. Lili was furious. She hoped that nobody had been injured. This made it clear to Lili once again that her jailers would not spare her life if push came to shove. She always tried to find something positive and this was no exception, it simply increased her resolve not to give up.

Dear Reader, I forgot to mention that in the first couple of days of her captivity, Lili and John had come to an agreement: if one of them asked a question that could not be answered, the person would say "No comment" and that would be respected. The other thing that she made very clear to him was that her captivity would have one of three outcomes: Her family would pay and she would be released, they would kill her, or she would not be able to cope with all the pressure and commit suicide. However, she told him under no uncertain terms that he could forget about the third outcome because she was not going to do the dirty work for them.

Lili finished knitting John's sweater, but had not as yet given it to him. That night she told him she had a present for him and handed him the sweater saying, "This will remind you of this day for as long as you live." He ignored her comment and simply thanked her. Needless to say, she never saw him wearing it.

Chapter 7

Lili heard over the radio one day that a lady had been kidnapped and she felt very sorry, being able to identify with her. Yet the poor thing was only just beginning her ordeal while she, Lili, was already well versed. Several victims had also been set free, one after seven months and another after 11. She therefore knew that her confinement would not end at least before September.

Knowing that she wouldn't harm herself, her kidnappers brought her a mirror so she could see what she looked like. Her reflection gave her a shock. Due to the lack of sunlight, she was extremely pale and her hair was black and peppered with grey. Her eyes filled with tears, but she did not allow that moment of weakness to last long and committed to not feeling sorry for herself, which she complied with. She would look at herself every morning and talk to herself. It was the only face she ever saw, besides the ones on *Time Magazine*, because her jailers were hidden behind masks.

Another time whilst listening to the news, she heard about the kidnapping and death of one of her classmates. Being the daughter of an ex-president, it had been politically motivated, having been held by a drug warlord. This had a huge effect on Lili. On one hand, feeling grateful that hers was only money oriented, it also showed that she had no guarantee of coming out alive.

In addition, her physical health was deteriorating. She no longer had the endurance to walk on her tray for an hour, but she forced herself to do it on a daily basis for forty minutes while listening to music. Exercising on her mattress was too exhausting for her and after reducing the time, she finally gave it up. She hated the thought of falling sick, but knew that

41

the lack of sunlight and Vitamin D as well as fresh air were affecting her. She convinced herself over and over again that she could not fall ill, since those gangsters would never call a proper doctor, and although they might have one among their ranks, the mere thought of one of them touching her made her want to throw up. Every morning, upon waking and feeling grateful for still being alive and that nothing untoward happened to her during the night she would order her body to stay healthy; and dear Reader believe it or not her body did as it was told.

Thoughts are free. Yes, her captors had her physical body at their mercy, but they did not have her subtle body. In her thoughts, she travelled to Lake Geneva and spent a great deal of time there, enjoying the mountains, the boats on the lake and relaxing on the terrace. Her daydreams would usually be interrupted by someone bringing her something to eat. She began spending more and more time daydreaming and this was probably one of the things that helped her the most. Lili also missed physical closeness, like being hugged. She had never given it any importance, and most of us are not aware of it, but to compensate she would lie in a foetal position and hug herself giving the feeling of the warmth she was craving.

After the rocket attack, things began moving along at a faster pace. John and Rose came in one day and told her they needed to send proof that she was alive. It would be a photograph. Lili's joy was short-lived. She was told to make up her face and arms so they looked as though she had been beaten and was given some blue and green coloured make-up. Since she didn't do a very good job of it, Rose did it for her. Then they said she should be crying in the picture. She refused, but John told her that if she didn't start crying, he would put lemon juice in her eyes and added, "…that will certainly bring on the tears."

Lili still refused, but when he told her the pictures were going to be sent to her daughter, she was horrified and the tears started flowing. The thought of her children and husband receiving those pictures and their reaction to them haunted her for days on end. Sometimes she just wanted to give up. She had a mirror which she could harm herself with, but her conscience would make itself be heard above the chatter of the monkey mind and point out that having endured so much already and that her captivity most likely moving closer to an end—it would be a great shame not to wait for the outcome. And of course, she reminded herself: *You cannot let them, or you, down!* She always, eventually, succeeded in bringing herself back to reality.

She was enraged with her kidnappers and would have loved to insult them, but she was well aware that it would not achieve anything, quite the contrary. Never having to see or talk to them was her wish, but then again, she was completely dependent on them.

They forced her to take a shower again, which of course she refused, but John told her that everyone was complaining about the stench. Rose was in the bathroom again, guarding her, and while she showered, Rose said that if she was planning on continuing her hunger strike and losing more weight, they would be obliged to feed her intravenously. John had threatened Lili at one point, saying that if she died, they would still ask for her ransom. But they would have to settle for less and he wasn't even sure they would return her body. This was a terrible thought. Her husband and children would have to live with the doubt of not knowing what her end had been. A friend of her family's once had met the same fate and his relatives kept hoping every day that he might show up, even though it had happened some ten years ago.

Lili's journal was her confidante. She wrote down every single detail of her conversations with John, also writing down what she thought the strategy to negotiate her release her husband might be using. It was like a game of chess and it kept her brain active. Her captors always gave her little bits of information, trying to provoke a reaction from her, but she never allowed herself to be drawn in, well aware that they were trying to get her involved in the negotiations. Yet again she was told that communication had broken down, which might force them to hand her over to another gang. This really frightened her, but knowing from experience that one statement was always followed by a contradiction, she tried hard not to let it affect her.

It was now summer in Europe. She could almost smell the air and it made her very nostalgic. What would the children be doing? Would they be leaving for the US as planned? She had no way of knowing. Looking back, her intuition had not failed her. She had been worried about not being able to attend her daughter's birthday party and boarded the flight to Europe in December, feeling as if she were fleeing some unknown danger, apprehensive about her return to Colombia. Yes, she had sensed the danger all along and deep down inside, prepared herself to face it.

She knitted, translated, and read *Don Quixote*; at one point, she wasn't certain if she was becoming like Sancho Panza, and imagining things. Her captors began calling her Maria Magdalena because she wept so much. Then she received a new guardian, a girl. When they first met, the girl asked Lili if she liked birds. Lili was surprised at the question. The girl did not wait for an answer, she just said, "You are like my little bird in a cage." The girl had no way of knowing, of course, that unlike the caged bird, Lili could fly away and leave her body behind.

Lili woke up one morning and remembered it was her husband's birthday. *How would he be celebrating it?* She wondered. *Would the kids have ordered a cake for him?* Suddenly she remembered that he had not been in a good mood at all on his last birthday and refused to have a birthday cake. She heard herself saying, "We take so many things for granted. We refuse one thing, or leave many things until later because we always believe there will be more time." She continued, "Do not leave anything for tomorrow, for tomorrow may never come." Then, "Be aware of your choices and choose wisely, for they only come once." Lili resolved that if she were to regain her freedom, she would live by this.

John entered and in an urgent tone of voice told her she had to answer some questions they had received. Lili was delighted, but she refrained from showing it. The questions could only have come from her husband. She felt so relieved,

44

maybe the end of her captivity was not so far off. John mentioned that if things continued at this rate she might be released by August. Lili thought about it, but she did not believe his words, her intuition telling her that this would not be the case. Once she had asked John why he was giving her a time frame and his reply was, "One always has to show the tiger that there is a way out." Lili thought about this and decided there was some wisdom to it, making the situation look less hopeless. *When one loses hope, one loses everything.*

The new girl brought Lili some fresh bed linen and washed her clothing. Having a clean bed and being able to change into clean pyjamas made Lili feel almost human again. The new girl, whom Lili named The Newcomer, had a very interesting story. Her family was poor and her mother washed clothes for other people, earning very little. She had studied nursing, then became a drug addict and got caught stealing from the hospital where she was employed. After she escaped jail, she wandered the streets until she somehow ran into John who helped cure her addiction and gave her this job.

One day the tall guy reappeared, a broom in one hand. He handed it to Lili and suggested that she swept her cell. She thought it an excellent idea, only to realise that she tired extremely fast and this worried her, although there was nothing, she could do about it. The tall guy mentioned matter-of-factly that she would not be leaving anytime soon, saying that the new President was being sworn in at the beginning of August and the city would be militarised so there would be no contact with the outside world. He also told her he was really fed up with the job and all he wanted was to go home and be with his family, but this would only be possible once she was released. He also mentioned that they had forbidden him to go out. Lili thought to herself that the bosses had taken this step-in order to prevent him from doing something drastic and placing them all in harm's way.

Every time someone came to speak to her, they told her a different story. Yes, the negotiations were going on... No, they were not offering enough... Yes, the communications had been broken, and only God knew when they would resume. All of this created a world of anxiety for Lili, but she did not take any of it to heart. Instead, she wrote everything down, reading and rereading, and saw the different contradictions, resigning herself to a long wait.

However, she did worry about them handing her over to another gang or killing her, but when she asked John about these things, he told her that those were not options, and they were all in the same boat. One had to be patient, for everything does pass. Yes, everything will pass...but when?

Chapter 8

Then, when she had least expected it, John came in and told her they had come to an agreement and that she would soon be a free person again. All they needed was to send more proof she was alive. They took two pictures of a smiling Lili holding a message, written by her and directed at her husband and children. In it, she announced her joy at being able to come home. It contained information only her husband could know and her intention with the message had been to prove to them that she could think and was mentally stable. The terrible looking guy came and told her that due to her good behaviour, they would be releasing her as soon as the funds were received. John said he hoped everything would go well with the payment.

Lili dared not think about what she would do once she was free. However, she did ask John to return her purse, then took out the pictures of the children she always carried with her. Looking at them after so long brought tears to her eyes. Now that she was leaving, she was bringing them into her captivity and pinned them onto the wall where she could look at them. Thinking about all the suffering and uncertainty they had endured pained her greatly.

A few days later, she was asked for her ring and was reluctant to surrender it, but John said he really needed it. She was still the merchandise and the investment, but once they had received the money, she was fully aware that she would no longer be of any value to them. This thought anguished her a great deal, but lately she had felt so very tired and exhausted that she didn't even want to leave her bed and it took all her willpower to do so. In fact, on one particular weekend she didn't ring for anyone, she just lay dozing and in her half-awake state, wondering if they would let her be or come in and check on her. John did come and ask if she was alright.

Shortly before the day she was supposed to be freed, John told her that some problems had arisen with the payment and that she would have to stay one week more. She did not say much. What was the use? It only took away what little energy she had left, and so she made up her mind to be there another week and began to organise her radio schedule for the weekend. Then, the next day, John broke the news to her: she would be allowed to go that evening.

Lili could not believe her ears. Overjoyed, she laid down and tried to imagine what it would be like to be free again. She also tried to imagine arriving home and seeing her family again after such a long time. But she was unsuccessful, having blocked everything out of her mind and feeling only pain and sadness. All she could do was look at her hands and resent that her ring had been taken.

By mid-afternoon, John said it was time to get ready to leave, and that she was to take a shower. This time she did not oppose it. The same procedures were followed as the other times and Rose was in the bathroom, of course. All she could talk about was how glad she was this job was over. Lili crawled into her cell for the last time and as she sat in her living room, she became very much aware that this life of doing nothing, of just being, was coming to an end. Her time of silence, and enjoying that silence, was soon to be left behind. She would go back to a world full of demands and noise. *Was she ready for it?* She wondered, and was sure it would take time. Looking back at those 269 days, which were ending today, she felt a sense of accomplishment that she had succeeded.

John interrupted her daydreaming by returning her clothes. She dressed, putting on her boots and jacket. Her feet would have to get used to wearing shoes again as she had gone barefoot for so long, and she desperately needed a pedicure. Repeating to herself time and time again that she was being freed, she still couldn't believe it. She looked inside her purse and placed the pictures of the children in her billfold. There was not a penny in it. John came in, folded up the mattress and left with it. It took him exactly half an hour to empty out her cell and leave it in the state in which she had first seen it. She asked him if he was going to leave the rest but he told her everything would be disassembled. Her cell had served its purpose and their mission had come to an end. They had been captives as well and now they were free to leave.

The tall lean guy told Lili he was counting the minutes before he got out of there, never to return, then said, "You know, I learned my lesson. It's better to be poor and a free man than to earn a good salary and compromise one's freedom."

They had left her to her own devices. She sat on the floor, wondering when the time to leave would come, when John entered and announced a visitor would be coming to see her. When he arrives, he said, she should stand by the gate with her back to it, looking at the wall.

She did as she was told, then heard a dreadful voice which made her stomach drop. In a very determined tone of voice—the visitor—a man, said, "You are being released today, right after we receive the payment. This is not how we normally operate. but we are making an exception. You behaved like a lady the entire time, and taking this and your health into consideration, the partners have agreed to your immediate release. I must warn you, however, should you play foul we will know about it. We are everywhere and you and all your family will be dealt with. I wish you good luck." After saying these words he was gone. Lili was stunned and hoped she would never ever have to see or listen to that man again.

Lili had told John that before she left, she would like to say goodbye to all those who had looked after her. They came in one by one and she thanked them and wished them well. When Rose asked her if she hated them, Lili replied, "I hold no grudges. You were only doing the job you had chosen."

She sat on the floor of her cell and looked around her. John nearly fell over backwards when he saw the gallons of water, rolls of toilet paper, batteries, chips, chocolates and wool she had kept hidden from sight. He just said, "You had supplies to last you for at least another six months." She watched him take everything away without replying to his comment. It was late and dark when he returned to tell her they were leaving. He handed her a pair of dark glasses, the same ones she had worn upon her arrival, and put them on. Someone carried her down the stairs, sat her in the backseat of the car and John took his place beside her. He mentioned that they were all armed and another car would be following them just in case. Before leaving the cell, he gave her some money so that she could get home. She was also to let her family know she was free. Lili was so very nervous. Her mind kept on a repetitive chant; *you are free! You are free!* to which her pessimistic side replied, *you are not, you will only be free once you are on your own.*

They hadn't been driving long when the car came to an abrupt stop and John told her to get out and start walking. Hearing the door slam shut and the car drive off, she took off the glasses and looked around. *I am finally free*, she said to herself once more. Her monkey mind began asking how she was going to get home to her family but she hailed a passing cab and got out a block from her house. Luckily, John had given her enough money to pay the driver.

She walked home feeling the excitement building up inside her. After 269 days in captivity, she was finally going to be able to hug her husband and children. She rang the doorbell and her eldest daughter opened the door, and then yelled, "Mama is home!" Everyone came running and it really was a very joyful homecoming.

She looked at the children; they had grown so much during her absence and seemed so mature while her husband had aged with all the worry. He could not stop saying how delighted he was to have a wife again. Everyone commented on how well she looked and that they could tell she was mentally fit, which she was. No one was in the mood to go to sleep. They talked until the wee hours, trying to catch up. But one cannot catch up on 269 days in one night, or even in one month. They watched the sunrise together, full of gratitude for being reunited again. The only cloud hanging over this joyful reunion was the knowledge of her father's passing. Once the children had gone to bed, her husband filled her in on the details.

Lili felt great sorrow and a huge disappointment. From the very first day of her captivity, she thought of sharing her ordeal with her father, telling him how she had handled it, thinking of it as if comparing notes, "I did this…what would you have done?" There would have been many similarities, she was certain. But while she had returned, he had departed this planet and although she knew she should be grateful that his suffering had come to an end, no amount of argument could fill the void she felt. Lili was unaware at that time that there was a letter awaiting her. I am sorry, dear Reader, but as usual I am getting ahead of myself. Please be patient, I will come back to this in due course.

Chapter 9

Lili was home, and yet she felt as if she were watching a movie. She received so much attention that her thoughts could hardly be heard over the clatter of chatter and noise. Longing for the silence, just being able to be, she realised that for now it would not be possible. She tried to get back into her routine, which turned out to be quite a chore since she thought she could just 'do it'. But the space, as I should call it, between the 269 days and the now could not be bridged. Lili came to call it the 'hole'. Time had not stood still for her family, they had continued living, whereas for her, it had been a vegetative state, let's say. No place to go, nothing to do, emotions completely banned, a blank face and no goals.

Her daughter made her aware of this by a little detail. She compared the colour of her hair to that of her mother's and said in a surprised voice, "Your hair is completely dark and it used to be blond, like mine!"

"That is due to the lack of sun," replied her mother. "One takes the sun for granted but now you can see how important it is." Lili slowly became conscious of everything she had been deprived of. Fully aware of the important things, she was beginning to realise the benefits of the little things she had been deprived of.

When she had been made captive, she'd had no choices, surrendering to the circumstances where there had been no options. Freedom entails not only choices but being a part of life. Part of life means not only sharing and caring but having emotions and being able to show them and act on them. She had made a point of switching off all emotions and now she would have to locate the switch and regain the capability to love—to feel empathy towards others. The iceberg she had